THERE'S
A BOOK IN HERE
SOMEWHERE

There's a Book in Here Somewhere

Insignificant events of my life

By Steve Bernstein

Illustrations by David Isaacs.

Design and composition by Lynne Adams.

These stories constitute a collection of my own memories and reflect my own experiences of people, places, and events. I apologize for any instances where my perceptions, as I relate them, might be construed as injurious to anyone mentioned or implied. I can only offer my apologies. As Robert B. Reich put it so well in his introduction to *Locked in the Cabinet* (1997, Alfred A. Knopf), "I claim no higher truth than my own perceptions. This is how I lived it."

ISBN 0-966-2602-3-6

34 Main Street, N° 6
Amherst, MA 01002
413-253-2353
www.modernmemoirs.com

This book is dedicated to Ilise, the best wife a man could ask for (cooking excluded), and my twin brother David, whose memory is far better than mine.

Left to
right:
Billy,
David,
Bobby,
Morty,
and me

Nana and Gigi

Brooklyn Bridge

standing: me, Morty, Bobby
seated: Billy, Norma, and David

Fredi, Daliah, and Carolyn

Gigi and Goldie

Ilise

Statue of Liberty

Contents

III. Me

IV. Work

V. Epilogue

Preface

The purpose of this book is to keep a record of all the stories I have experienced, enjoyed, and repeated countless times over the years. Once published, I may never talk again. I will just hand someone a copy of the book and walk away.

I am sure that as my friends and relatives read this book, I will get many comments and corrections. I can hear them even now: "It wasn't a blue car, it was a red car." "We were sixteen years old, not fifteen." The point is, Who cares? This is how I remember it. It's not a legal brief. The flavor of the story is important, not the minute details. Two people often look at the same picture and see completely different things. My advice: Don't critique it—just enjoy it.

There are some stories in this book that I am not entirely proud of. Actually, I am proud of the fact that, in most cases, we never got caught, never got beat up, and rarely got punished—but some of our behavior was clearly inappropriate. We were each fortunate enough to have had a good sense of judgment and we knew when to call it quits. In Brooklyn, it's called "street smarts." Many things that we did as children would be viewed differently today and if my children behaved the way I did, it would be very upsetting. I am certain that if my parents had known about all of our actions, they would have felt the same way. So consider this an open apology to all the people we might have wronged. It was all meant in fun and I hope you got over it to be living full and prosperous lives. For a good number of you, I would bet against it.

I

FRIENDS AND NEIGHBORS

CAN WE DUST?

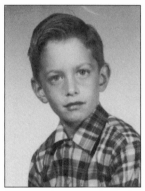

Me at eight years old, 1969

After school and on weekends, my twin brother David, our friend Andrew, and I used to go up to apartment 4H to see Nana and Aunt Goldie. It was fun to hang out there and play with the dogs and feed the bird (while it was alive). Many days, we would help Goldie with the housework. This allowed her more free time to smoke the Chesterfield nonfiltered cigarettes that were more necessary to her than water to a fish. The housework we usually did for her was to dust the shelves and all the nooks and crannies. We really enjoyed it, although I am still not sure why. At eight years old, it doesn't take much to make you happy. Maybe we enjoyed it because it gave us a chance to hold all the valuables, which we were typically told not to touch because we would break them. Whatever the reason, we liked to dust. We liked it so much that we had what we thought was a great idea: We would go to other people's apartments and ask if we could dust for them!

We started at an apartment down the hall in which an old couple lived with their two rat-like dogs. The husband, Al, was always friendly to us, but the woman wasn't. To us, she looked like a Volkswagen with breasts. We knocked on the door. There was no answer, but we kept trying, and we finally heard a woman's voice shrieking, "Just a minute!" We had been hoping Al was home, but it was too late to turn back now. His wife opened the door and my friend Andrew and I said, in unison, the fateful words that I am still embarrassed about: "Can we dust?"

"What?" she squawked, looking very annoyed. She was dripping wet and had obviously jumped out of the shower; it was not a pretty sight. "Can we DUST?" we said again, with more of an attitude this time. That's when the screaming started. "I'm gonna tell your mothers on you! Go away from here! Don't you have anything better to do?"

Sadly, we didn't.

SNOWBALLS AND A GUN

It was an early winter evening and we must have been around thirteen years old. Andrew, David, and I were out in front of our apartment building, throwing snowballs at passing cars on Ocean Parkway. Again, it seemed like a good idea at the time, but as frequently happens, the decisions of youth are not some of the brightest ones. One of us let loose a snowball and it was timed perfectly (that means I probably threw it), sailing right over the service road and onto the roof of a car on the parkway. As we whooped it up, I noticed the car making a right turn at the corner. Probably no big deal, I thought, but just in case, I kept my eye out for a car coming around the left corner. Sure enough, about one minute later, a car turned into the service road and headed towards our building. I had a bad feeling that it was the guy we'd hit, coming around the block, even though it was too dark to see the car clearly.

I started backing up towards the lobby of the building, but Andrew and David continued throwing snowballs. I warned them that it might be the same guy. David showed some caution and backed up halfway, but Andrew was in his element and didn't move a step. I was in the lobby when the car stopped in front of the building and a man jumped out and pointed a gun directly at Andrew. I have to say, this was the first time I had seen a real gun, let alone been remotely threatened by one. Andrew must have been a first-timer as well because he was paralyzed with fright. He couldn't move. He was like a squirrel caught in the headlights and just stood there as we yelled, "ANDREW, RUN!"

We could have run into our apartment, which was just off the lobby on the ground floor, but felt the man could've gotten off a clean shot, so we bolted up the stairs to Nana and Goldie on the fourth floor. As we flew into the apartment, my heart was pounding out of my chest. I just kept thinking, how would I explain to Andrew's mother that he had been shot because of a snowball I threw? I didn't even speak Ukrainian! I breathlessly told my grandmother that a man was pointing a gun at us. Of course, I left out the part about the snowballs as I didn't think it would help our situation.

She did what any Jewish grandmother from Brooklyn would have done. She went over to the window, looked down at the man and screamed, "Go 'way, go 'way from here ya bastard!" He eventually did. My grandmother, my hero.

THE WALLET TRICK

I always loved practical jokes, except if they were directed at me, and we had some great ones. We used to stand on opposite sides of the street and when a car came down the block, we'd brace ourselves and pretend to be pulling a heavy cable with all our might. If the driver caught sight of us, he would screech to a halt and yell at us to drop the rope. We would give him a perplexed look and just walk away. My favorite joke was the wallet trick. It was simple, but very effective, as it played upon a person's greed. The greedier they were, the better it worked.

Basically, you took the corner off a twenty-dollar bill and taped it into an old wallet so it looked as if the money was coming out of it. You then tied fishing string to the wallet, sat about twenty feet away, and started "fishing."

We did this countless times and it worked like a charm. As soon as the person bent over to pick up the wallet, *whoosh!* We pulled it away. It left people thoroughly embarrassed and us in hysterical laughter. Frequently, the person didn't realize what was happening and would try to pick it up again. *Whoosh!* We would get them twice.

One afternoon, my brother David, and friends Jeff, Alan, Rich, Rob, Daniel, and I were sitting on Ocean Parkway and decided to play the wallet trick. We sat on the benches in front of the house, which were separated from the bicycle path by a low metal railing. We set the wallet down on the bicycle path and jumped over the rail to position ourselves on the far bench. Sure enough, a group of five innocent girls about our age (fourteen) were riding their bicycles towards us. They were close together in a group and, fortunately for us, the one who was in front turned out to be the greediest of them all. She spotted the wallet and slammed on her brakes immediately, without regard to the four girls behind her.

CRASH!!! Before we knew what was happening, there was a pile of twisted metal and groaning girls. They had all landed on top of each other. A perfect strike. As we were doubled over in hysterics, the pile suddenly started to move and the lead girl started crawling towards the wallet. She was determined to get that wallet, no

matter what. She loosened herself from the wreckage and reached out for the wallet. *Whoosh!* Alan jerked the wallet back towards us. When she realized what had happened to her, she was livid and so were the other girls. We felt it was best to find a safer place to laugh, so we ran through the park and never looked back.

The very next day, Rich and I were walking home from our friend Ben's house. We were side by side and deep in discussion of what I'm sure was some trivial event when greed took over. The next thing I knew, we both went diving for a wallet that lay in front of us. We elbowed each other out of the way as we fought towards our reward. As usual, at the precise moment of seizure, *whoosh!* The wallet disappeared into the mail slot of a private house. Foiled at our own game! How could WE fall for it? We were very embarrassed as we walked away to the sounds of snickering coming through the mail slot.

A CONSIDERATE GRANDSON

It was my friend Jeff's grandmother's birthday and Jeff must have been about twelve years old at the time. He loved his grandmother. Everyone did, as she was a lovely lady. Jeff wanted to buy her a nice present, so he went by himself to a department store on Kings Highway to pick out something special. Jeff hunted around for the perfect gift and finally settled on a bottle of perfume; at least for a twelve-year-old boy, it must have looked like perfume. It was actually a very intimate feminine hygiene product. He brought it to the counter and proudly asked the cashier to have it gift-wrapped.

"Are you sure?" she replied, probably thinking Jeff was either very advanced for his age or totally clueless.

"Yes, I'm sure. It's for my grandmother," he said.

The clerk shrugged and gift-wrapped the item because at $3.00 an hour, she wasn't paid enough to explain the vagaries of feminine hygiene to a twelve-year-old boy. Jeff ran home, excited to give his grandmother the special present.

Well, that he did. Grandma was mortified, his mom freaked, and I am sure the clerk wasn't too happy when he returned it a few hours later. As for Jeff, he still gets teased about it, twenty-five years later.

THE CAMPBELL'S SOUP JINGLE

As kids, David and I were often alone in our apartment because my parents were at their store, the Silver Mart, and Billy and Bobby were off at college. This wasn't a bad thing—it gave us a chance to do many things we couldn't get away with if anyone else was home. One of our favorite pastimes was taking out the *White Pages* and making prank phone calls with Jeff and other friends.

We would choose some helpless victim from the phone book and usually Jeff, David, Andrew, and I would huddle together on the two extensions. We tried all the old favorites, like "Prince Albert in a Can" (you call the supermarket and ask if they have Prince Albert in a can, and if they say, "Yes," you respond, "Then you'd better let him out!") and "Calling Mr. Bigger" (we'd look up the last name "Bigger" in the phone book, call a man with the last name "Bigger," and ask, "Who is bigger, you or your son?" and then we'd say, "We think your son is just a little Bigger").

But the one we liked the best and had the most success with was "The Campbell's soup jingle." Luckily for us, there was no such thing as caller ID back then, or we might have been phoneless and bored silly—you can only do the wallet trick a few hundred times before it starts to get old.

The gag went like this: "Hello, this is Bruce Sawson of WTFM radio, 109.3, the Big Sound in the Big Town. We are calling up listeners and asking them to sing the Campbell's soup jingle for us. If you can, you

will receive one, I say ONE CASE, of Campbell's chicken noodle soup."
David was always the radio personality, as he had the best rap. It still
amazes me that people could mistake a prepubescent teen with a high-
pitched voice for a radio announcer, but greed tends to cloud a person's
judgment.

In case you forgot, the jingle went like this: "Ummm ummm good,
ummm ummm good, that's what Campbell's soup is—ummm ummm
good." True, it's not very catchy, but it got its point across.

As we usually remember our successes and not the failures, my memory tells me that it worked quite often. Here are some of the better ones.
It started off the same every time....*Ring*....*Ring*....

Mr. Parks: Hello?

David: Hello, Mr. Parks? Hello, this is Bruce Sawson of WTFM
radio, 109.3, the Big Sound in the Big Town! Can you sing the
Campbell's soup jingle for us?

Mr. Parks: Well I'd just like to say that Campbell's pea soup is just
about the best soup I ever tasted.

David: OK, pea soup it is.

We howled for hours.

After they correctly sang the jingle, we offered the suckers a bonus
round. They could win another case of soup if they made up their own
jingle.

We called Mr. Gene Glantz of Brooklyn, who sang slow and steady,
"I...like...Campbell's...soup...because...it's the best soup that is
made...how about that!" He was good, but he still never got his soup.
We couldn't even afford a can of soup, let alone two cases.

The best of all was Jack, who went by the nickname of Bubba and
everyone knew as (and still is, as I write this) the neighborhood bookie.
He inherited the job from Sol (the Tuna) Katz, who was loved by everyone except the guy who pumped four bullets into his chest. That's how
Bubba got the job; that's probably also why Bubba never left the house.
It was Bobby's idea to call Bubba because it was a sure thing he would
answer the phone—it was his umbilical cord.

David: Hello Mr. Brooks? This is Bruce Sawson of WTFM radio,

109.3, the Big Sound in the Big Town! Can you sing the Campbell's soup jingle for us?

Bubba: Can you hang on a minute? [You know how bookies are—anything to get the edge. We heard Bubba rummaging through his kitchen cabinet looking for a can of Campbell's soup so he could read the jingle off the can. He must have been successful because he came back on the phone with an air of confidence.]

Bubba: Can I recite it?

David: No, you have to sing it.

And sing he did. We collapsed with laughter. Bubba also was lame enough to participate in the bonus round. (His new jingle was to the tune of *Home on the Range*.) "Caaampbell's soup is so gooood. I eeeat it e-ve-ryyy dayyyy." It was classic. If I have one piece of advice for Bubba, it would be to definitely try and get out of the house more often.

HOLY WATER

Every kid likes throwing stuff off a roof to watch it fall and listen for the thud. We took it a step further: We hunted. Our weapons were usually eggs, but this day we used water balloons.

Jeff, David, and I went to the roof of the synagogue near Jeff's building. With limited ammunition, it was critical to find the right target, so we watched. We waited. And it was worth the wait. A smartly dressed, middle-aged man hurried past the front of the building and right into our trap. We let loose a barrage of water balloons; some of them hit him and others exploded around him.

He was not a happy man. After a few shakes of his fist and some graphic superlatives, he dashed into the building to come up after us. Trapped, you might think? Give us more credit than that! We didn't choose the roof of the temple to be closer to God—it happened to have two staircases, so as he ran up the front one, we bolted down the back.

While he was on the roof, peering down at us, we were on the sidewalk, laughing up at him. He knew it was over at that point. His only weapons were words, which only got more colorful and were entirely inappropriate for a house of worship. We lobbed some more water balloons up at him and did what we did best—ran away.

EGGCITING

For us, throwing eggs from the roof of Jeff's building was as enjoyable as a trip to Disneyland would be for my kids. It was also a lot cheaper, especially if we stole the eggs. We usually paid for them, but once David did steal a package of bacon and threw it off the roof after a long barrage of eggs had pinned some pathetic souls in a doorway. I would have loved to see their faces when, after being pelted with eggs, the package of bacon landed at their feet. David should have added some orange juice and a few slices of toast to make it a complete breakfast.

We usually tossed eggs from the top of Jeff's apartment building, which had six stories and a very large roof. The problem was that it had two entrances into the lobby but only one stairway leading to the roof. That made escape difficult. I didn't like the odds.

I didn't actually participate in the episode I remember the best. David and Jeff headed up to the roof, expecting me to come along, but for some reason I had a bad feeling about it and decided to stay in Jeff's apartment and watch from his bedroom window. This was the defining moment in my life, when I learned to trust my instincts. They proved to be correct. I turned off the lights in Jeff's bedroom and reclined on the bed with my head facing out the window; I wanted a bird's-eye view but didn't want to be spotted when the angry victims searched for their attackers. I was excited and anticipated a good show, and was not disappointed.

Not long after they went up to the roof, a beautiful white convertible with a red leather interior stopped at the light. It was driven by an Italian stallion in his early twenties. He had his arm around his babe and the music was blaring. He must have thought he was King of the World. Sorry, Your Highness. Before I saw the first egg pass by the window, I knew this guy was a goner. The eggs were right on target. They landed in the back seat, the front seat, and all over the hood. There was no place to hide.

The guy was royally pissed. He started cursing and reached into the glove compartment. His girlfriend tried to calm him down but he pulled out a handgun and wildly pointed it up at the building. Just my luck, I thought—the one time I am NOT involved, I get shot anyway. I drew back from the window, and what seemed like seconds later, Jeff and David came bolting into the apartment, scared to death. We locked the door, turned off all the lights, and for the next hour sat perfectly still. We knew this guy was coming after us. The only advantage we had was that there were over 100 apartments in the building. I was just afraid that he'd spotted me in the window. Fortunately, the only thing we eventually heard were the sounds of Jeff's brother coming into the apartment.

It was the second time we faced a gun, but we had no doubt that this guy would have used it. After that incident, we stayed on a low-cholesterol diet for awhile.

Jeff, thirteen years old

LOUIS THE PAPER BOY

With a family of four boys (two sets of twins), you can imagine that stepping into our apartment was not usually a relaxing experience. It certainly wasn't for our hapless paper boy named Louis. Louis was twelve years old, which put him about four years younger than David and I. That also meant he was easy prey. It didn't help that he was about thirty pounds overweight, with a big, cherubic face, cute in a trollish sort of way. Why he would ever step back into our apartment again, after the first time we tormented him, I will never understand. Some people feel any attention is better than none at all. We took full advantage of his weekly visits to collect the money. If Mom was home, Louis usually got away relatively unscathed, maybe just a noogie or two. When we were alone, he would have been better off leaving immediately and paying for the paper out of his own pocket. This probably would have added a few years onto his life.

One particular day, Bobby and Billy were home from college, so Louis had all four of us to contend with. Bobby came up with a trick to play on the unsuspecting news carrier. We stuffed, sealed, and addressed an envelope and told Louis it was the last letter our grandmother had ever written, so it desperately had to be mailed today. We asked him to mail it for us on his way home; he gladly agreed. We warned him many times that it was very important and to be extra careful with it. Louis stuffed it in his back pocket and was getting ready to leave. We had been relatively nice to him on this visit because we knew the gag was in play. Just before he left, Bobby said, "Come on Louis, let's see how tough you are," and started to wrestle him to the ground. As Louis was about to be pinned to the floor, I reached into his back pocket, took the envelope, and hid it. As Bobby held Louis down, we took turns pinching, flicking, and pulling his nose. This dazed him. When he stood up, we ushered him out the door. As we expected, he completely forgot about the letter. We figured he would remember it about an hour later and crawl back to us, begging for forgiveness. Our idea was to berate him for awhile, show him the letter, and then torment him some more.

It didn't quite work out that way. Louis finally remembered about the letter when he got to his grandmother's house. He panicked and told her he had lost this very important letter. He must have been beside himself because for the next two hours, Louis and his grandmother retraced his whole paper route, looking for the missing letter. It was snowing incredibly hard that day, which made their search all the more miserable. Later that evening, after we had completely forgotten about Louis, his grandmother called to say that she was extremely sorry, but Louis had lost the letter. She said they had been looking for it ever since, but with no success. Although we had wanted to wind Louis up, we felt bad that Grandma had to trudge all over Brooklyn during a blizzard, with her overweight grandson, searching for a nonexistent letter. She probably saw Louis's future career as a postman going up in smoke. We calmly told her on the phone that Louis must have dropped the letter in our apartment before he left, and assured her that everything was OK, and apologized to her for going to so much trouble for us. She hung up the phone, probably thinking we were the nicest and most considerate bunch of boys.

We were no less surprised to receive an invitation to Louis's bar mitzvah a few months later. We didn't attend the affair, but mailed him a check anyway—we told him that if we handed it to him, we were afraid he might lose it.

THE PHONE BOOTH TRICK

Jeff, eighteen years old

Today, some kids have the ability to hack into the most sophisticated computer systems in the world. Sixteen-year-old boys have been arrested breaching security firewalls of the Pentagon and other government agencies. When we were sixteen, our biggest feat was making long-distance calls without paying for them. We used to call the American embassies in various countries and ask to speak to the lance corporal. Sometimes we would dial the Soviet embassy and demand that they accept the call or be in big trouble with the Kremlin; then, our friend Larry, who had emigrated from Russia, would take the phone and demand in Russian that they cooperate or face the consequences.

In order to participate in this free form of entertainment, all we needed were two phone booths side by side. Across from Jeff's apartment building was our favorite spot. We would call any number we wanted from the public phone and charge a collect call to the phone next to it. (We'd figured out very early on that all phone booth numbers have a fourth digit as a nine. Most of the operators, apparently, were not clued into this significant detail.)

I used to carry a list in my wallet with about twenty phone booth numbers throughout Brooklyn. Anytime I made a call, I used to charge it to one of the booths. Sometimes they required a party to accept the call. No problem, as usually Jeff or David were standing right next to me and would gladly accept the charges. We did this for years with great success. This even lasted through college. One time I was on the phone to New Orleans for over two hours because I bet against Tulane in a college football game. My old girlfriend was a student there, so I called her and she gave me the play-by-play from her TV, all on Ma Bell's dime.

One day, we were outside Jeff's building and had been making random calls for hours when we spotted a police patrol car coming down Kings Highway. Growing up in Brooklyn taught us to keep an eye out for trouble. We ran around the block and hid behind the corner of an apartment building. Sure enough, the police car stopped at the phone booth, looked around the area, and picked up the phone. I'm glad they didn't dust it for prints. We got away just in time or we'd have been making our last free phone calls from the 65th Precinct.

Another time, David and Daniel were on adjacent phones on Avenue P. They purposely started insulting the operator to keep her listening in after connecting the call. Then they started graphically describing fictitious crimes and murders. Shortly after they hung up and walked away, five police cars converged on the corner and started asking the shop owners if they had seen any suspicious characters nearby. Asking that question in Brooklyn is clearly overstating the obvious.

The phone booths outside Jeff's building were visible from Jeff's living room window. We would watch from the window and call it when we thought some random passerby would answer it. When they picked up the receiver, we would tell them they shouldn't have picked it up, as the phone booth was rigged to explode, so they had better run. If they got cute with us, we would describe their clothing, so they knew they were under surveillance. A few guys actually bolted. We laughed like hell.

MARTY

HOME RUN FOR MARTY

Marty was the neighborhood kid with the bright red hair and freckles; a staple of every neighborhood in America. Most of us have grown up knowing someone like Marty, the carrot-topped boy who was always picked last for every softball game. Marty didn't get picked last because of his hair color or because of the annoying grin he always wore—we were more fair than that. He was picked last because he was a terrible softball player. I mean, really awful. He couldn't hit the ball out of the infield and Helen Keller would have made fewer errors with a glove.

Marty always got to play, though, because he had a key advantage: He would always bring the bat and ball. That guaranteed he played. No Marty, no bat and ball. No bat and ball, no softball. He was actually a nice kid, otherwise we probably would have chipped in for another bat and ball and told Marty to shove off. Sure, he weakened any team he was on, but at thirteen we cared more about playing than winning.

Marty wasn't the problem. His father was the problem. His old man came with Marty to every game. Back then, we never questioned why he wasn't at work—he was just a fixture every time we played. Sometimes this made us feel guilty, so we would pick Marty second to last instead of last, which was a real insult to the one left for last. "How could you pick MARTY over me?" was usually his response.

In the game, Marty could do no wrong. I don't mean to suggest that Marty played well. Marty never played well, but that's where his old man came in. Every time we played, Marty's father was the umpire. If Marty got one of his better hits, which was a weak foul tip, his father would proclaim, "Home run for Marty!" Despite our protests, the game wouldn't continue until Marty bashfully trotted around the bases to our complete silence. After a while, we realized it was pointless to argue and it became a natural part of our games. Marty would dribble one to the pitcher. "Triple for Marty!" his father would proudly announce. He'd strike out. "Double for Marty!" he'd beam.

During our childhood, Marty reached more bases than Pete Rose. That was probably why Marty started to get picked a little higher in the order. We knew he would always get on base. We were smart enough to follow the rules. No base for Marty, then no Marty. No Marty, then no bat and ball. No equipment, then no softball. It was a small price to pay.

TRICK OR TREAT FOR MARTY

It was Halloween, probably 1974. Marty was out trick or treating by himself, probably collecting a bag full of rocks, like Charlie Brown. Andrew and David were hiding in the garden in front of the building—with a dozen eggs, of course. For Andrew, Marty was "a target-rich environment," as they say in the military. They egged him without mercy and he ran home, crying "I'm going to tell my father on you!" David wanted to leave, but Andrew wouldn't allow it. A few minutes later, an angry mailman (Marty's father) came striding down Ocean Parkway. "Where are you bastards that threw eggs at my Marty?" Dead silence. Strategic. He paced angrily around in front of our apartment building; Andrew and David were frozen in the garden behind the central bush.

Finally, he cursed and started to leave. After he took about ten paces, Andrew ran to the edge of the garden and landed a perfect egg on the back of his head, then slipped back into the hideout, frozen once more.

MONEY FROM MARTY

When I was a kid, two of the more exciting things were getting something for free and getting mail. I would check the mailbox religiously hoping for that one special letter addressed to me. If it wasn't my birthday, the chances were close to zero. Since we liked baseball, David and I used to write to baseball teams asking for free bumper stickers, decals or anything else that they would send. We told Marty about this and he was enthused. We also told him that for money we would give him the secret address of the New York Mets. He gave us a whopping TEN BUCKS and we gave him the address, *New York Mets, Shea Stadium, New York, NY.*

That night, his mother called ours.

DANIEL

Daniel was one of our more colorful friends. In fact, his whole family could be called interesting. Daniel had six brothers and one sister (who was a cop). They lived in a large house on Ocean Parkway, across from our building. None of us were ever allowed into his house. The closest I ever came was to be led into the basement, where I spotted a chalk outline on a wall of a man who had Chinese combat stars stuck in him. After that, my desire to visit his house lessened dramatically. Daniel's father looked exactly like Tex Antoine, who had been a famous weatherman on TV until he was bounced from the screen for making inappropriate remarks on the air.

Daniel himself was a bit of a rebel. When short hair was in style, Daniel wore his hair long. When the seventies came around and long hair was hip, Daniel got a crew cut. The Chinless Wonder (as his sister affectionately called him) was very smart and had a great sense of humor, which would always keep us amused.

I LIKE *YOU*, BUT I DON'T LIKE *YOU*!

We went to a party that somebody from high school was having and brought Daniel along. He attended a different school and wasn't going to know anyone there, but he was sure to liven things up. We walked into the living room of the apartment and immediately noticed a set of identical twin girls sitting on the couch. They were dressed exactly alike and looked identical, with bright red hair and freckles. Without hesitation, Daniel walked directly up to them, pointing at one, then the other, and exclaimed, "I like *you*, but I don't like *you!*" They screeched back in unison, "But we're twins!"

BELLY UP TO THE BAR, BOYS

McSorley's Ale House is undoubtedly the most famous Irish bar in Manhattan, so you can imagine that on St. Patrick's Day, the place was a zoo. Daniel insisted on going there for St. Patrick's Day one year, as it would be a perfect place to meet drunken women. The Chinless Wonder liked the odds. He had no fear; he would walk up to any woman seated at a bar, place his elbow down, and say, "Come on, I'll arm wrestle you for a drink." Most times, he lost.

McSorley's was mobbed and there was a line around the corner to get in. Against my bitter protests, Daniel insisted that we wait. We stood on line, inching slowly towards the entrance, for over an hour. We could only get in if other people exited and that didn't seem to be happening. When we finally approached the door, I was grateful to be able to see inside, even though it looked like there was no room to stand. Daniel was ahead of me and as he stood in the doorway, he spontaneously yelled, at the top of his lungs, "Belly up to the bar, boys, 'cause the drinks are on the house!" A huge roar emanated from the crowd and the place went wild. Commotion reigned and Daniel was the catalyst. The bouncers weren't pleased and threw us out of the bar. Actually, I hadn't even gotten a chance to step inside.

SUMMER CAMP

ANDY BINDELL

Every June, David and I left the concrete confines of Brooklyn for eight wonderful weeks of freedom at summer camp. We went to a few different camps, but stayed at Camp Impala for five great years. David, Jeff, Isaacs, Lance, Sidelle, and I started as campers and left as a group of inept counselors and waiters. On the first day of camp, we would meet the bus at Canarsie Pier for the long ride up to Woodbourne, New York.

This particular year, we were very excited as we were now CIT's (counselors-in-training). CIT's were nothing more than glorified campers. We still had to pay to go to camp and weren't mature enough to be responsible for anything, but we could boss around the little kids, so it was highly enjoyable.

As we waited on the pier for all the campers to arrive, we noticed the usual commotion coming from the Bindell family. Andy Bindell was refusing, as he did every year, to get on the bus. Andy was a small boy, about twelve years old, with a mop of very curly blond hair; he looked like a miniature Harpo Marx. His parents tried everything to make him comply: They promised him toys, they threatened him, they told him he only had to stay for half the summer, and, finally, they physically tried to force him onto the bus. All to no avail. His white knuckles gripped the edge of the door, with no intention of letting go.

It was time for the CIT's to get involved. We talked with Andy and tried to calm him down. We talked about the great things we'd do that summer. He wasn't buying it. We offered to let him ride up to camp in the CIT van with us. No dice. Then, with his parents' consent, we grabbed the little brat and forced him onto the van. At first, he fought for dear life. Then suddenly, he relaxed his grip and calmly got into the van. Success! or so we thought.

This little twelve-year-old was no fool. He got into the van, quickly jumped out the driver's-side door, and ran down the pier into the marsh. David was in hot pursuit. It was a scene straight out of the movies. Andy disappeared into the high weeds; David was a few seconds behind him and also disappeared from view.

Moments later, David came running out of the woods like a bat out of hell and Andy soon followed, swinging a very large branch menacingly from side to side. We couldn't help David, as we were laughing too hard. We finally were able to disarm Andy and force him into the van. Of course, he ended up having a great summer and we had a story to tell for life.

THE FLYING FUTZ

One summer, our camp counselor was a guy named Seth Zaglin. He was very cool and we got along great with him. Seth was short and dumpy, with a big bushy beard, and he always wore Earth Shoes©. Sports were definitely not his forte. He did have one skill, though, and for this feat we called him The Flying Futz. A flying futz is similar to high jumping, except Seth used campers instead of a bar. He would make a camper lie facedown on the bed with his hands at his sides, and then pile us on top one at a time. He would start at the back of the bunk and run full speed (for him, anyway) and dive headfirst over us onto the next bed. He did this often and after a while we got to like it, except if you were on top. I think his record was five campers.

My other memorable story of Seth was when one rainy day we left camp to see a movie. As he went away to arrange payment, we waited in the lobby. He warned us to behave, so we went straight to the phone booth and started making phony phone calls. Being that time was short, we decided to play a little trick on Seth. We called information and requested the phone number of the Zaglin residence in Brooklyn— fortunately for us, his last name was not Cohen. Having memorized the number, we waited for Seth to return. When he returned, I pretended to hang up the phone and we all started to laugh. He, of course, wanted in on the joke. I concocted some story about making a prank call to some woman and really winding her up. I said she didn't have a clue what was going on and we'd made her crazy. He had a big smile on his face and started to laugh along with us. I said, "We should call that old hag again. I even remember her number, 212-636-8308." We could see his mind starting to process the familiar number and the smile slowly dissolve from his face. His eyes widened and he blurted out in a panic, "HEY, THAT WAS MY MOM!" The Flying Futz crashed and burned.

Heads up!

When we were young, our summers were spent in Mount Freedom, New Jersey. We called it the country house because anything outside of Brooklyn seemed like the country to us. On weekdays, we attended Jefferson Lakes Day Camp. It was a large, well-run camp and it kept us out of our mother's hair every day, for what I'm sure were a few grateful hours. The camp director was a pathetic soul who we were forced to call Uncle Dudley. He demanded attention when he was speaking and had a certain procedure for it: He would yell "HEADS UP!" and make a peace sign with his fingers, holding them high in the air. All campers were obligated to repeat this silly ritual and stand quietly at complete attention.

One afternoon, there was a big intercamp softball game going on. Our group was sitting in the bleachers, fooling around and not paying particular attention to the game. We were picking on Noodles, who was the group's resident nerd. I swear he was the first person to wear thick black glasses held together by white adhesive tape. I think the name Noodles basically sums him up. Anyway, as the game progressed, the batter hit a high foul ball on the third-base side. As the ball descended onto the bleachers, one of the counselors yelled out to warn us. "HEADS UP!" he screamed. Poor choice of words. As we all dove for cover, Noodles thrust his peace sign high in the air and yelled proudly, "HEADS UP!" ...SMACK! the ball hit him square in the head. Because he was the only one yelling, everyone saw it happen, which made it worse for him and better for us. If I ever see Noodles again, I am going to yell "HEADS UP!" just to see his reaction. He'll probably dive for cover while making a peace sign.

MILK

The cows are up in arms,
They've left their fields and barns,
They're marching from their farms,
Because kids don't drink enough milk.

Most kids, at some point in their lives, try to be the world's best at something. It could be that they made the biggest rubber band ball or became the youngest pilot to solo across country. For us, it was never that grand. Our biggest challenge was beating the camp record for drinking the most cartons of milk during lunch.

The standing record was twenty-one quarts of milk between ten campers. David, Jeff, Isaacs, Ira, Lance, Schweydock, three other idiots, and I decided that the record needed to be broken; we wanted to make camp history. We ate light. We skipped liquids at breakfast. We trained hard. And we were ready. The big decision was, Should we stick to the traditional plain milk or diversify with the better-tasting chocolate milk? We decided it should be drinker's choice. I went for the chocolate.

I was nervous—I didn't want to be the weak link. Our goal was two quarts of milk each, which was a lot for kids who barely weighed eighty-five pounds.

At the start, it was easy. We couldn't believe the record had stood so long. This was going to be a piece of cake. Actually, cake probably would have been a good idea. The milk started to go down a lot slower after the first few glasses. After one quart, it started to get painful, but we had to press on. Some of the guys started to look a bit green, but none of us wanted to be the one to fold. The whole camp was looking on as we struggled through the twenty-second quart. A new Camp Impala record!

I remember it was tough to get excited about it at the time because I was so bloated that I could barely walk. We stumbled out of the dining room and onto the black asphalt driveway.

That's when the first domino fell. Jeff puked a flood of milk all over the black tar. As soon as Ira saw it, he lost it also, then Schweydock, and so on. It was fairly easy to see who went for the chocolate milk and who stuck to nature's own. Fortunately for me, I was the first one out of the dining room and had bee-lined straight for the bunk, so all the white-washing happened behind me. I only glanced back once because I knew that if I saw it, I would either join them or turn into a pillar of salt. I lay down on my bed and didn't move for two hours. I don't think I had another glass of milk for a week.

COLLEGE

How Isaacs spent his summer vacation

David Isaacs, eighteen years old

We were all jealous. David Isaacs had lucked out with a great summer job the summer before college. He was going to be a caddie at the prestigious Winged Foot Country Club. That meant fresh air, sunshine, and the potential for big tips. I had nothing more glamorous lined up than wrapping packages and stocking the shelves at my parents' store, the Silver Mart. I enjoyed working there, but anyone would prefer being at a posh golf course and hobnobbing with the rich. Isaacs certainly did and he let us know it. Every day. He was relentless. "I'm going to meet babes, I get to play golf, and the money will be great," he smirked. We could do nothing but envy him.

His first day on the job, Isaacs was carrying the bags of two serious golfers. They were betting on every hole and the competition was fierce. Since the only thing Isaacs knew about golf was that there were approximately eighteen holes, he was of little help to the twosome and was basically told to stay out of the way; the relationship between Isaacs and the golfers soured when he left three clubs on the previous hole and had to run back for them. Meanwhile, the match was very close. With one hole left to play, it was even and the stakes were being raised. They were betting more money on a single putt than Isaacs would make all summer.

One of the players had a thirty-foot putt for birdie. Isaacs was standing by the flag, probably thinking of how big a tip he was going to get. As the putt started to roll towards the hole, it was dead on line and looked for sure to go in. The man screamed at Isaacs, "Pull the flag! Pull the flag!" Isaacs tried to lift the flag, but it wasn't cooperating. It seems that pulling it out on an angle just doesn't work well. "Pull the Goddamn flag out!" the man screamed, in desperation, when the ball was within five feet of the hole.

Isaacs panicked. He straddled the hole, grabbed the flag with both hands, and pulled up with all his might. The flag came flying out, but so did the cup and a huge mound of dirt surrounding it. The ball stopped dead in its tracks, blocked by the new hazard.

Needless to say, the event changed the course of Isaacs' summer. He was immediately fired and within two days was working in lower Manhattan, operating a dirty freight elevator in one-hundred-degree heat. No more babes, no more tips, and no more fresh air. What he did get was very sweaty and a lot of grief from us.

DEAN DONOR

Me, eighteen years old

It was freshman year of college 1979 P.I. (pre-Ilise) and I had been at Boston University (BU) for just about two months. I remember getting my mail one day and opening an ordinary letter from the School of Management (SMG). Inside the envelope, though, was something that caught my interest. There was an extra sheet of BU stationery. It was blank but had the official headings. To you, this may not sound like much, but I immediately saw the possibilities of a great practical joke. Now, I only needed a victim.

I went back to my room and on the way passed Larry Abrams in the hall. Bingo! Larry was a friend of mine (and still is to this day, believe it or not). He was a business major and acted the part—he was "Mr. Junior Achievement" and looked like he wore a three-piece suit to class. I knew nothing about business classes. I did, however, know a lot about practical jokes.

Gags are only fun if everyone is in on them, except the unsuspecting mark. I solicited help from my roommate Steve, his girlfriend Mary Beth, Scott (Larry's roommate), Gary, Dave, and Jerry. We thought of Jerry as the resident drug addict; if you didn't see Jerry high, you didn't see Jerry. With this stellar example of higher learning in place, we hatched a plan. I took out the school directory and looked up the Head of Student Affairs; he was listed as Dean Donor.

Then we typed a letter from Dean Donor to Larry Abrams. The letter stated that, due to Larry's superb academic record in high school, as well as his exemplary performance so far this year, he had been chosen to represent his class on the school's Academic Affairs Board. This was a significant honor, as only one student from each graduating class is selected. The letter asked Larry to get in contact with Dean Donor, Monday through Friday, between the hours of 10 a.m. and 5 p.m., and listed the Dean's office number. Of course, it wasn't really his office number. It was the phone number to Jerry's dorm room.

Since it was Friday at about 3:30 p.m., we knew Larry would not wait until Monday to call. We all went to Jerry's dorm room, as Scott handed Larry his mail with the letter included. By this time, there were about ten of us in Jerry's room, waiting for the call. I had a tape recorder hooked up to the phone so that we could record the conversation. Shortly after Scott made it back to Jerry's room, the phone rang. Mary Beth picked up after three rings and declared, "Dean Donor's office." "Hello, this is Larry Abrams. Is Dean Donor in, please?" Larry asked with an air of confidence. Jerry got on the phone and exchanged pleasantries with Larry. He asked Larry if he was excited about the appointment and was he going to accept it. Mr. Junior Achievement wanted some more information. Jerry was sketchy with the details, but said Larry should come to his office the following week to discuss it.

After he hung up, we listened to the tape a few times and then went down to Larry's room to wind him up. Larry was beaming from ear to ear. He started to tell us all about his new role. We feigned excitement and asked if he'd be joining us in the cafeteria for an early dinner. He said he would catch up with us after he called his parents. That was the last thing I wanted! We all pressured him into joining us for dinner and to call his mother later and he reluctantly agreed. All through dinner, we peppered him with questions about his new title and talked about how he could help us in the future. He had very few details to share, but it was clear he was proud.

After dinner, I asked Larry to come into my room because I had a tape I wanted him to hear, but he declined and started to dial his parents. I begged him to come and listen to just one song first as everyone was in my room waiting to hear it. He clearly didn't want to, but maybe he felt that with his new responsibility on the Academic Affairs Board, he should mingle with the masses.

The room was packed with people when Jerry walked in, smoking something. We were ready to begin. Larry sat on my bed across from me as I played the tape of his earlier conversation with Jerry, aka Dean Donor.

It was an amazing thing to watch Larry's face in the midst of all the grins surrounding him. As he listened to Mary Beth's voice, along with Jerry's and his own, his smile began to fade into astonishment. He started to shake his head slowly, from side to side, and muttered, "I can't BELIEVE you guys...I CAN'T BELIEVE you guys...I CAN'T BELIEVE YOU GUYS...TAPPED THE DEAN'S PHONE!"

I laughed for weeks and Larry didn't talk to me for days. Larry still has the original letter and I have the original tape, so if you don't believe me, I'll play it for you.

SERGEANT WARD

Being the thoughtful and considerate person that I am, when my friend Larry asked me to help him drop his car off at one in the morning at a garage in Framingham, I was only too happy to comply. I followed him in my car and our plan was to drive back together. The streets were deserted and the ride to Framingham took about twenty minutes.

I was driving behind Larry when a car suddenly pulled next to me and started honking the horn. I looked over to see the white face of a skeleton, peering at me from the driver's side. Being that it was pitch black outside and deathly quiet, I freaked. I pulled up to the traffic light and stole another glance at this creature. He now appeared like a normal guy, driving by himself, staring straight ahead, and taking no notice of me at all. I looked around, but there were no other cars on the road besides Larry's. Something was strange. After we started driving again, the honking started and I turned to see the guy waving his arms out the window at me with a skeleton mask on.

Having composed myself, my only thought was that this guy had picked the wrong person to play a joke on. I had to make him suffer. I copied down his license plate number, took a note of the car type, and started to plan. If this guy was out for a bit of fun with his friends, I would have laughed it off as a funny joke. What bothered me about this loser was that he had been alone in the car. As I said before, practical jokes are only funny if you share them with others. Playing them by yourself is like being the only one in the stands at a football game.

The next day, I called the Massachusetts Department of Motor Vehicles and explained that I worked at a service station in Framingham and had rebuilt a transmission for a guy, but he'd never come back for the car. I pleaded for the name and address of the car's owner. The woman from the DMV refused, saying she was not allowed to release that information. So I laid it on thick, saying that I did $2,500 worth of work on the car and my boss would fire me if I couldn't get the owner to come in. She finally relented and told me what I needed to know.

Armed with this information, I then called the Framingham Police Department and asked who the sergeant in charge was. It was Sergeant Ward, but he was on vacation in Hawaii this week and would be back the following Monday. All the better!

After connecting the tape recorder to the phone, I gathered my friends in the room. Posing as Sergeant Ward, I called the premises where the car was registered and spoke to a woman, who nervously put her husband on the line. I asked him if he owned a white Chevrolet with the license plate 463-BRF. He informed me that it was his son's car. I explained that we had a report of driving to endanger, possibly DWI (Driving While Intoxicated) and menacing. I asked to speak to the owner of the car, as the charges were serious and could result in a two-year prison sentence and up to a $5,000 fine. He said he had not seen his son in over a year and wasn't sure where to reach him.

I wasn't buying that. I started to commiserate with him. I told him I had a son about the same age and that it is difficult to control them sometimes. He started discussing his problems with his son and asked me if I could cut him a break. I told him I'd think about it and would call back that afternoon at three p.m. (after class, of course). I warned him that I expected his son to be there; he assured me he would.

Shortly after three p.m., we contained our laughter and I dialed the house. On the first ring, the prankster answered the phone. I asked him to identify himself, which he did. I explained the charges to him and the seriousness of the offenses. He apologized profusely and said he had not been drunk but was just trying to have a little fun. I started to explain that his idea of fun could have had serious implications, as any car accident that resulted from it could have cost lives; he was lucky not to be facing a charge of attempted manslaughter. He promised never to behave this way again and said he now realized how foolish he'd been.

I was thoroughly enjoying this moment. I was about to curse him out and surprise him with the fact that it was yours truly in the car, but I wanted to make him sweat a bit more. I said that his father seemed like a nice man, and because of that, I would cut him a break. I ordered him to come down to the Framingham Police Department first thing Monday morning and I would arrange some community service work for him as punishment. He was extremely grateful, as was his father.

After I hung up, we all sat around laughing and tried to picture this guy waiting for a well-rested but sunburned Sergeant Ward to assign him community service work. I never called back and I erased the tape because, as you know, impersonating a police officer and wiretapping are serious offenses.

II

FAMILY

NANA

Nana, Bobo, and me at the summer house in New Jersey

Most of us have funny stories about our grandparents. Keep in mind that one day, we will be the ones whom stories are told about.

My maternal grandmother, Nana, was a joy. She was the first woman I ever saw drink a beer and her cursing would make men blush. She had lost her husband early in life and raised two children, by herself, while running a successful business (Silver Mart). She was a tough, no-nonsense woman with a heart of gold. She was also a piece of work. Here are just a few examples.

THE CHINESE BROAD

Nana in Japan

My grandmother ran the Silver Mart from her perch behind the cash register, which was at the desk in the front of the store. From there, she could guard the cash and at the same time keep an eye on everything. After customers gave their orders to the saleswomen, Nana would bark the order over an intercom to my father and his obedient flock of stockboys, who would quickly wrap the package (with no regard for aesthetics) and walk it out to the desk.

One day, a client purchased a beautiful porcelain figurine of a Japanese woman dressed in a kimono and holding a bouquet of flowers. One of the stockboys brought the gift-wrapped package to the front desk, where a number of people were waiting for their purchases. My grandmother tried to identify the purchaser in her soft, mellifluous voice. "WHO GETS THE CHINESE BROAD?" she screeched, "WHO GETS THE CHINESE BROAD?"

Nana did not see the Chinese woman who happened to be standing by the desk, waiting for a package of her own. The woman was mortified and had no idea how to react. When someone pointed out to my grandmother this Asian woman's look of distress, she cackled, with a cigarette dangling from her mouth, "Don't worry, sweetheart, I'm not talkin' about you."

SORRY, LADY...

Since we lived in the same apartment building as my grandmother, it didn't make a lot of sense for her to drive to Silver Mart by herself. For the most part, my father was her regular chauffeur. After closing the store, Nana used to wait outside while my father went to get the car. One bitterly cold day, she was waiting on the corner for my father to drive up. She had been standing there for quite a while, and as she would have said, she was freezin' her ass off. She kept looking down the street for Mort's station wagon, but it was nowhere in sight, which did not please her.

Finally, a station wagon pulled up to the corner and stopped at the light, and Nana got in, cursing a blue streak. "Where the hell were you? Don't you know I'm freezin' my ass off out here?" she bellowed, while settling into the backseat.

A very startled black gentleman with a good sense of humor turned around and exclaimed, "Sorry, lady! I didn't know you were waiting for me! Otherwise I would've been here earlier!"

I LOOK UGLY TODAY

Nana

Nana was out to dinner at an upscale restaurant with my parents and some friends. They were waiting for a table in the lounge and Nana was pacing back and forth, trying to keep busy, as she was not one who liked to be kept waiting. She looked into the mirror and remarked, "Boy, I look ugly today." That may have been true, but it wasn't a mirror that she was looking into, but a glass window with another heavyset, white-haired woman peering through from the other side.

BACKSEAT DRIVER

Every morning, Nana would wait outside the building for my father to drive her to Silver Mart; if it was cold, she'd sit and wait in his car. One year, Nana decided she wanted her independence so she bought a new car and started to drive herself to work.

The first day proved difficult. She was so used to being driven to

The first day proved difficult. She was so used to being driven to work that, since it was very cold that morning, she opened the car door and got into the backseat. She waited there for twenty minutes, cursing loudly the fact that my father was late, before she realized that it was her own car and the driving responsibility was hers.

STEVE BERNSTEIN

GOLDIE

Gigi and Goldie

Goldie in her kitchen

FULL OF LIFE

Writing about my grandmother's sister, my Great Aunt Goldie, could be a book in itself. Never have you met a person so full of life (and girth). She had a special bond with all of her great-nephews and -nieces, as she related to us on our own level. Describing her is fairly simple: She was an obese woman who chain-smoked nonfiltered Chesterfields and whose usual choice of attire was an old blue housecoat. She had a great sense of humor and always reminded me of Jackie Gleason with breasts. She shared a large apartment with my grandmother, but rarely left the small kitchen, which was usually crowded with dogs, birds, and a television that never seemed to be off. That barely left room for her.

***

We used to go up every day to say hello and play with the dogs Goldie loved and my father hated. I remember one time when Nana and Goldie were getting ready to leave for the summer house and Goldie put all of Nana's jewelry into the elevator with her dog Gigi, and pressed the button for the lobby.

Nana almost had a stroke when the elevator got stuck between floors, but Goldie was sure that Gigi, a fat, mentally retarded (but sweet) poodle, would guard her treasures.

Goldie was always fun to joke with. Later in her life, when she was in the hospital, Bobby went to visit her and asked if she needed any money. Her eyes lit up. She probably wanted to stockpile a few more cartons of cigarettes. Bobby took out four $20 bills and placed them between Goldie's toes. He told her that if she could reach them, she could have them. Being such a large woman, she was barely able to see them. She couldn't stop laughing, which turned into a coughing fit as tears of happiness streamed down her face.

***

A practical joke I once played on Goldie didn't work as well as I hoped. I had been in a joke shop and purchased exploding flints that you put into someone's cigarette. The flint was supposed to make the end of the cigarette explode, leaving the smoker a bit distressed. This gag had "Goldie" written all over it.

There was only one problem. When I tried to put it in Goldie's cigarette I realized that she smoked Chesterfield nonfilters. I had no idea which end went into her mouth, but I figured I'd try my luck. I put the flint in and kept a close eye on her as she fished the cigarette out of the pack. True to form, she put the "loaded" side into her mouth! I had visions of it exploding in her mouth much like a *Looney Tunes* cartoon— I couldn't let her go through with it. As she started to light the cigarette, I quickly reached out and snatched it from her mouth. Taking a cigarette away from Goldie was not an action to be taken lightly. No sooner did I have the cigarette in my hand than Goldie had her nails embedded in my forearm. A cobra couldn't seize its prey that fast! Try to explain to a lifelong nicotine addict that you are taking away her much-needed fix, then factor in that she weighed three times as much as I did, and you can understand my concern.

MORT

Mort in the Silver Mart

If you know what I mean....

My father has a way with words, to be sure. In order to make his point, he will often repeat himself six or seven times. If you don't acknowledge him, you could get stuck on the same point for hours. He would be a terrible air traffic controller.

One of his more memorable conversations was with my friend Lee. Since Lee was a CPA and small business owner, my father used to discuss the Silver Mart and its related business practices with him. Lee would get cornered into discussing purchase orders from Rainbow Ribbons or some other gift-related supplier.

One afternoon, Lee was discussing bookkeeping with my father and asked a simple question, "Do you have an accountant?" True to form, my father lets out a small sigh, shakes his head slowly, and repeats, "Do I have an ACCOUNTANT? Do I have an ACCOUNTANT? I HAVE an accountant, but I DON'T have an accountant, if you know what I mean…"

Lee and I howled with laughter because we had absolutely no idea what he meant, but my father thought he was being perfectly clear. I knew an explanation was coming. It seems that my father's accountant was serving time in jail for fraud, so technically he had an accountant, but he didn't have an accountant, if you know what I mean.

MORT'S FAVORITE DOG

My father had an interesting relationship with animals. If they were on TV, he couldn't get enough of them. God forbid you talked during Mutual of Omaha's *Wild Kingdom*. You would be ordered out of the room immediately. My father also had a special bond with Marlin Perkins, the show's host. Marlin would explain the dangerous feat that Jim, his lackey, was about to undertake, while he himself was perched safely in the studio. My father would sit safely in his chair, grunting the occasional, "Quiet already!" as if we were disturbing the animals.

As much as he loved watching animals, Mort couldn't stand it when my Aunt Goldie's dogs were in the apartment. If they happily trotted over to his chair and started sniffing him, he would scream, "Go 'way from here, Goddammit!" He showed them no affection whatsoever. I never saw him pet any of the dogs even once. A gentle kick would be all the effort he'd muster.

This drove Goldie crazy. One day, when we were having a large family dinner, Goldie turned to my father and asked, "Morty, of all the dogs I ever had, which one did you like the best?"

Expecting him to show his disgust, we were all shocked when he quickly said, "Bo-Bo."

Goldie beamed with pleasure. You could see the joy in her eyes at Bo-Bo being my father's favorite. She cooed, "Oh, Morty, why Bo-Bo?"

My father looked her straight in the eye and replied coolly, "Because he's dead."

I wonder what Marlin Perkins would have said.

IF YOU'RE *LOOKING* FOR A GOOD TIME, YOU'LL *HAVE* A GOOD TIME...

Norma and Morty, decked out for an affair

I was fourteen years old and it was our cousin Adam's bar mitzvah. Adam wasn't really our cousin, but our families were very close and we always used the terms uncle, aunt, and cousin. We spent a lot of time together, as my Uncle Stan was and still is my father's best friend.

My parents were very excited about the bar mitzvah.

My brothers and I were less so. We liked Adam a lot, but schlepping all the way out to Long Island to sit in temple dressed in a polyester leisure suit was not our idea of fun. The party would be full of our parents' friends, hovering all over us, asking the same twin-related questions over and over. "So who's older?" "How many minutes apart are you?"

For the record, David is older by two minutes. No matter how many times people ask the question, it doesn't seem to change the results.

We were not shy in voicing our discontent at the idea of attending a sacred event like this. Bobby always took it a step further. "I'm not going," he'd defiantly say to my father. "Oh yes you are," my father would threaten. Of course, everyone knew Bobby would have to go, but he still had to inflict a little pain.

My father's mood started to soften when he had us all trapped in the car. He tried to talk us into the fact that we might actually enjoy ourselves. "IF YOU'RE *LOOKING* FOR A GOOD TIME, YOU'LL *HAVE* A GOOD TIME," he said hopefully. And he said it again. And he said it again. He repeated this mantra all the way to Hewlett, which took an hour. At times, there would be dead silence and then out it would come: "IF YOU'RE *LOOKING* FOR A GOOD TIME, YOU'LL *HAVE* A GOOD TIME."

It must have worked because we actually did have a good time. But Mort didn't. My father is not much of a drinker. Coca-Cola is more his speed than anything alcoholic. If he's feeling adventurous, he might add a slice of lemon. Well, needless to say, he got caught up in the moment. He was probably happy that his kids stopped complaining and he had a night out, and proceeded to get smashed in very short order. He spent practically the whole reception sick in the car with his head out of the window, like one of my Aunt Goldie's dogs. At one point, I went out to the parking lot to check on him. He looked miserable, but I couldn't pass up the opportunity: I strolled over and said, "Dad, are you OK?"

He grunted; he was having trouble speaking.

I said, "You know, if you're *looking* for a good time, you'll *have* a good time."

He mustered up the strength to give me one sloppy, "Get the hell out of here," as I hurried off eagerly to inform my brothers about his condition.

THEY'RE GOING TO SOUTH AFRICA

1624 Avenue U (corner of East 17th Street), Brooklyn, New York

Stuey worked for my father in the Silver Mart for many years and had the illustrious job of gift wrapping packages and stocking shelves. Stuey didn't possess an advanced degree in quantum physics, but he was a loyal, trustworthy individual, much like the Saint Bernard that carries a flask around his neck in case you need it.

One afternoon, Stuey returned from lunch and walked by the front desk where my mother (and grandmother before her) would sit and ring up the sales. Norma was engaged in a conversation as Stuey walked by and overheard an obese woman telling my mother she'd be going on vacation to South Africa in a week's time. He strolled into the back and saw my father speaking with a gentleman who was one of my parents' longtime customers. Introductions were made and Stuey eagerly joined in on the conversation because, let's face it, thirty-year-old stock boys don't enjoy much personal interaction.

After a few minutes, the man said to my father, "Yeah, and we're going to South Africa for vacation next week." Stuey turned to the man and blurted out, "That's funny, the pig in the front is also going to South Africa next week." It hadn't occurred to him that the "pig" was this gentleman's loving wife. My father turned as white as a piece of fine china and, needless to say, Stuey's chances for career advancement at the Silver Mart were about as far as Brooklyn is to South Africa.

HE DON'T KNOW ME

Fred Harris is a famous artist in Japan. His paintings are known for their lifelike Japanese imagery. What is interesting to me is not that he has lived in Japan for over twenty-five years and speaks the language fluently, but that he is originally from Brooklyn, NY. He grew up in Brownsville, near my father, and is about the same age as him.

Since my father never forgets a name or a face, I decided to see if he remembered a person named Fred Harris. Instead of just asking him outright, I thought I would have a little fun, though. I called my father in Florida and put him on the speakerphone so that my friend Art could listen. I told my father that I'd met someone from his old neighborhood who was now living in Japan.

"He says he knows you," I lied, hoping to pique his interest.

"What's his name?" my father asked gruffly.

When I mentioned the name "Fred Harris" and that he was a famous artist, he quickly reached his conclusion. "He don't know me. He don't know me. He's connin' ya. He's trying to sell ya a picture."

I tried to explain that Fred Harris was very famous and didn't need to make up a story about Murray Bernstein in order to sell a picture. Mort wouldn't buy it. Since he remembers everyone he ever met in his entire life, it would be impossible for Fred Harris to know him and my father not remember it.

NORMA

Norma and Morty

OUR MOTHER'S DAY POEM

It was a Saturday night, just before Mother's Day. Billy was away at law school in California and my parents were out for dinner. Since none of us—Bobby, David, nor I—had bought a Mother's Day card, we decided to write a poem to pay homage to our dear mother. We also wanted to get a howl out of it. This is how it started:

Eye of Lizard, Teeth of Newt
Moo of Cow and Zigbeast snoot
Our language is strange as we babble of beasts
and are not very appreciative of your gourmet feasts.
Pizza for Goldie, whitefish for Mort,
We salute you with a Mother's Day snort.

Seven or eight classic verses followed, but we have long since forgotten them; we never really got a chance to memorize it because we showed the poem to my father as soon as he and Mom got home. Without saying a word, he tore the sheet of paper into pieces. A Hallmark card would have been a better idea, but certainly a lot less fun.

Until I had children of my own, I never really appreciated what my mother had to go through raising two sets of twin boys who were only four years apart. When I tell people about my sibling status, almost everyone says, "Your *poor* mother!" Now I understand.

In a house of five males, it was necessary for my mother to be tough—and tough she was. She would yell at us, "Just wait until your father gets home!" and we'd be wishing the same thing because she actually had full control of the home front and seemed to know what we were up to at any given moment.

***

One time, when I was nine years old, I didn't make it home to the bathroom in time, and soiled my pants. I was afraid to tell Mom, so I went directly into my older brothers' bedroom and changed into a pair of Bobby's pants. I was hoping to slip by her undetected. No such luck. She was reading a book but when I tried to scurry past her with a quick "Hi, Mom," she looked up and immediately noticed my pants, bunched up over my shoes, with me holding up the waist with both hands. Her exclamation, "*What* are you *doing?*" still rings in my ears.

Like most boys growing up, we pushed the limits to see where her breaking point was. Believe it or not, I was not the perfect son. I remember once kicking a hole in a plasterboard wall because Mom turned the television off abruptly (after calling me eight times for supper). Did it matter to me that she took care of all the household chores and then went to the Silver Mart for a full day's work, only to rush home to cook dinner and clean up after us? Apparently not. It must have been a very good cartoon.

***

One time, I got very frustrated with Mom about a trivial issue and blurted out "Fu— you, Mom!" She was sweeping the kitchen floor at the time and as soon as she heard that, she picked up the broom, wielded it threateningly over her head, and came after me. She chased me out of the kitchen, through the living room, and back through the kitchen. This went on for what seemed like hours, with me pleading, "I'm sorry!" over my shoulder, at every turn. Fortunately, I was slightly quicker than she was and she didn't catch up to me. But she did get the last laugh. After circling the kitchen and living room for many laps, she started to giggle. I thought she finally saw humor in the situation, so I slowed down. Mistake! she caught up to me and bashed me with the broom more than once.

***

An incident I still regret occurred when David and I were at summer camp. I was a rebellious fifteen-year-old and hadn't written home all summer, so Mom wrote a sarcastic note to me, saying how nice it was to receive all of my letters and to please keep them coming. My response? I ripped her letter into pieces and mailed them back to her in an empty envelope. Sorry, Mom.

***

There were a few times when we actually tried to do something nice. My mother has always been a heavy smoker, so one time David and I tried to persuade her to quit. We cut the Surgeon General's warning label off her multiple cartons of cigarettes and placed them all over the house, from the refrigerator door to under her pillow. She did quit for brief periods, but our behavior undoubtedly forced her back to the comfort of nicotine. It is amazing we never drove her to drink.

***

When I graduated from elementary school, my mother penned a memorable phrase in my autograph book. She wrote, "Although you are part of a pair, you are one of a kind." Now, so many years later, I realize it is she who is truly one of a kind.

LOLA

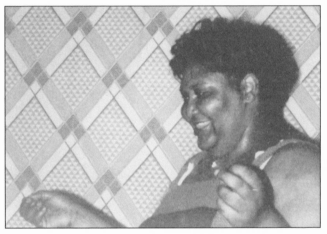

Lola in our Brooklyn apartment

Lola, a very large woman of color, was our housekeeper for most of our childhood. She would come to the apartment twice a week to clean. Having been raised in Anderson, South Carolina, she had a great southern drawl and would squeal a long, "OOOOOOOOOOOOOOO OOOOOOOH!" whenever something pleased her. She was also hilariously funny. Once, after our friend Jeff left our apartment with his new Israeli girlfriend, Lola commented, "There ain't enough ugly girls in America—he's got to import one?" If Lola didn't feel like coming to work, she would think up clever excuses, like her bellybutton hurt.

***

When we were eleven years old, David and I were playing cops and robbers. David, who was the cop, was searching for me all over the apartment. I was hiding in the closet when, plastic gun in hand, David kicked open the door of the bathroom and screamed, "POLICE BUST!"—only to find Lola, stark naked, in the process of changing her clothes. "DON'T YOU COME IN HERE!" she wailed at him. I think it was the last thing David had in mind.

BILLY

Billy, 1977

THE ALTERCATION

Billy was driving home from Syracuse University one morning and caused a minor fender bender when he smacked into a car driven by an elderly man with a heavy Italian accent. They exchanged licenses, along with other relevant information, and agreed to get in contact that evening, after they had spoken to their respective insurance companies.

Our Uncle Dicky has always been a fantastic storyteller and practical joker. He had heard about the accident and decided to have a little fun at Billy's expense. Dicky called the house and asked me to put Billy on the phone but not to tell him who was calling. In a heavy Italian accent, Dicky started screaming something along the lines of, "You break-a my car, I break-a your face!" and "I mind-a my own-a business and all of a sudden, *a-Boom!*"

Billy tried to maintain his composure. He had no idea it was Dicky on the other end of the phone, but my parents, brothers, and I were all watching him and trying to suppress our laughter. I almost lost it when Billy calmly said, "Sir, I am sure we can resolve this altercation."

Then Dicky cut him off and snapped back, "Alteration? Alteration? I am notta tailor!"

At this point, Billy lost his composure and screamed, "I can't talk to this idiot!" and threw the phone across the room.

IS THIS A DAGGER WHICH I SEE BEFORE ME?

Billy and Bobby had just started their freshman year at Syracuse University, which would put David and myself at fourteen years old. My father was very excited because Billy and Bobby were going to call home every Sunday night at 8 p.m.; this was to be the first try. My father likes things organized and working smoothly, so he warned us fifteen times, in his endlessly repetitive style, not to use the phone because Billy was going to call. This seemed like another perfect chance to play a joke on our unsuspecting father.

I remembered having a cassette recording of Billy practicing his part in a high school production of *Macbeth*—we used to listen to it and make fun of him, as he sounded so ridiculous being from Brooklyn but talking like an aristocrat from sixteenth-century Scotland. "Is this a dagger which I see before me? Its handle towards my heart? Come. Let me clutch thee…."(This is the only phrase from Shakespeare I remember, even now.)

David and I went into the bedroom and set up the tape recorder with Billy's *Macbeth* speech paused and ready to play. I called the operator and told her we were having trouble with our phone—could she please ring us back? She was happy to comply. The phone rang twice before I gently picked it up and quickly thanked the operator for her help. Moments later, my father picked up the phone in the kitchen, expecting to hear Billy or Bobby, as it was just eight o'clock. Our father's "Hello" was greeted with Billy's voice saying, "Is this a dagger which I see before me?"

My father responded, "Billy! How are you Billy? How's school?"

To which Billy replied, "Its handle towards my heart? Come, let me clutch thee."

This went on for a while, with my father getting more and more aggravated, and finally yelling at Billy to quit fooling around. He soon realized he should have been yelling at David and me.

BOBBY

Bobby, 1977

It should be noted that my older brother Bobby is the most responsible person I know: If you ask him to do something for you, then consider it done. His twin brother, Billy, is basically the opposite: If you ask him to follow up on something, then you had better call and remind him. Bobby is extremely neat and overly organized: He leaves money out for the cleaning lady two weeks in advance. Billy's cleaning lady has to rummage behind the couch cushions to make bus fare. Bobby's compulsive habits do not make him the easiest person to live with—Billy can attest to that, as they shared a bedroom for more than eighteen years. I still remember when Bobby padlocked his albums so that none of us could borrow them without his permission. (I used to wriggle them out from under the chain.)

Here are some stories to prove that it is not always preferable to be neat, efficient, and organized.

BOBBY AND MOM'S JEWELRY

Besides being well organized, Bobby was extremely neat. Everything had a place and it drove him crazy to share a room with Billy, who under ordinary circumstances would be considered neat, but not compulsive. Since we lived in Brooklyn, and therefore crime was a way of life, our mother often found creative ways to hide her most valuable jewelry, including many precious family heirlooms.

This time, she had hidden it in a plastic soup container, stuffed with paper towels, and placed on a high shelf in the kitchen cupboard. Ordinarily, this would have been a perfect hiding place, but Bobby was on a cleaning binge. My mother had just returned from a bar mitzvah and had put the jewelry she'd been wearing back into the plastic soup container, with the rest of her best jewelry, and left it on the kitchen table for a few minutes while she went into the bedroom to take off her makeup. All of her jewelry of any value was packed into the plastic soup container.

As is the case with most misfortunes, a moment of carelessness turns into a lifetime of despair. Bobby decided it was time to tidy up the kitchen. Mistaking it for a plastic soup container with some discarded food in it, he threw the plastic soup container into the garbage.

In most houses, losing jewelry this way meant that you had to rummage through the garbage can to retrieve it. Not so in our apartment building. All of the garbage was burned in an incinerator, which happened to be running at full flame as Bobby tossed the bag in.

Minutes later, my mother returned to the kitchen and quickly pieced together what had happened. She was completely distressed, of course. But it was difficult for her to figure out how to yell at Bobby—how *does* a mother yell at her son for being too neat?

BOBBY'S AIR CONDITIONER

Always a creature of habit, Bobby would put his air-conditioning unit in the window on Memorial Day (May) and remove it on Labor Day (September). It didn't matter what the weather was like; he was compelled to make the change.

One extremely hot Labor Day, Bobby asked me over the phone to come to his apartment and help remove his air-conditioning unit from the window. He mentioned that it was brand new and quite heavy. I asked him if he realized it was 100 degrees Fahrenheit outside and wouldn't it be better to wait until the weather cooled off? We argued back and forth for a few minutes. Finally, I told him I had better things to do than remove a one-hundred-pound air conditioner in the blistering heat.

Bobby cursed me out and took the task on by himself, but when he lifted the window to loosen the unit from its location, he did not keep a firm grip. The oversized unit fell from the window, thunderously crashing into the courtyard below, leaving pieces of plastic and metal strewn about. Bobby peered out of the window, assessed the situation, and closed the window of his sweltering apartment without uttering a sound. Then he called me and cursed, profusely.

DAVID

David, 1977

THE FISH TANK

It is a fact that David had read more books before the age of sixteen than I will read in my entire life. I am talking about real books, such as those written by Ayn Rand, Joseph Heller, and Franz Kafka, among others. To quote my father, "What David forgot, you'll never know." My activities as a youth were much simpler. Every day, as David was reading, I would head out to the park to play basketball, paddleball, or stickball. I would return and he would still be reading. The problem for me was that when it rained, I was bored to tears, while David's life was unaffected. This would cause me to get a little restless.

One rainy afternoon when we were fifteen years old, I was moping around the apartment and wanted David to stop reading and play with me. He was lying on his bed in the room we shared, absorbed in a book and showing no desire to stop. I kept pestering him, and at some point I took a basketball and tossed it at him, knocking the book from his hands. This infuriated him and I saw in his eyes that he was ready to retaliate. I enjoyed getting David riled up, but didn't want to pay the consequences, as he was stronger than I was. I bolted out of the room just as David took the basketball and drilled it at me as hard as he could. He missed, of course, as all those years of reading had done little to improve his hand-eye coordination.

As I ran from the room, I heard the basketball careen off the doorframe, followed by a loud crash and a torrent of running water. I ran back, half-knowing what had happened: the basketball had missed me but smashed our twenty-five-gallon fish tank, which was now pouring its contents of water, gravel, and fish onto our new shag carpeting that my mother had recently ordered for us.

I pinned all the blame on David and said, "Mom's gonna kill you," knowing I had to set my story straight early. The fish were bouncing all over the shag carpet as the water dissipated, leaving a pile of wet, smelly gravel to clean up. I went for the vacuum cleaner as David started scooping up the half-dead fish. The vacuum didn't work as well as I'd hoped; the gravel was too heavy to be sucked up and the water wasn't cooperating, either. But it did manage to inhale a few guppies. We spent all afternoon on our hands and knees, wading through the soggy carpeting and picking out bits of gravel and fish we had overlooked. This was not how I'd wanted the afternoon to turn out, but it did cure my boredom.

THE CRAB TRAP

When we were about fourteen, David, Andrew, and I went to Sheepshead Bay one day to poke around the piers and hope something exciting would happen. It was very cold and not many people were out. We were goofing off at the end of the dock when I spotted a rope tied to the pier, its other end in the bay. I reached over and pulled up what turned out to be a crab trap with some small crabs inside.

David and Andrew were extremely jealous at my find; even though I'd have to return the trap because it belonged to someone else, I could at least play with it for a while. They scoured the dock to find a trap of their own, but had no luck.

Then, Andrew peered into the water and saw a metallic cage glimmering from the bottom of the bay. He reasoned that it must be an abandoned crab trap whose rope had been lost. If they could retrieve it, they would be able to keep it for themselves. I peered over the edge of the dock to confirm their find, and then it was I who was jealous, because if they could get it up to the surface, they'd be able to take it home with them.

As the trap was at least ten feet down, it would not be an easy task, but Andrew had an idea. At the next pier was a large fishing boat with the captain aboard, preparing it for the next day. Andrew and David went over and sadly explained that the rope connecting their crab trap had fallen into the bay and thus they could not retrieve it—would he be kind enough to let them borrow his gaff to pull it back up? Since the fisherman didn't want to see his gaff join the trap at the bottom of the bay, he volunteered to help.

He peered down at the shiny object and asked, "Are you sure that's your crab trap?"

"Oh, yes," David replied with confidence.

The thoughtful seaman lowered the gaff into the water and quickly hooked the trap. Then he pulled and pulled, but it wasn't moving. "Are you POSITIVE it's your crab trap?" he implored, straining his muscles at every tug.

"Yes, we're sure!" Andrew asserted.

The man continued to struggle and finally dislodged it from the depths of the bay. After fifteen minutes of tug-of-war, he was sweaty and tired. He inched the trap slowly to the surface.

"It must be full of crabs!" Andrew exclaimed, hoping the explanation would ease the captain's burden.

Just then, what turned out to be a very old metal shopping cart broke the surface of the water and the word "Waldbaums" was clearly visible on the red handle. The Captain was livid. As he struggled to free his gaff, we ran from the pier as fast as we could.

ON THE LOOKOUT

It was a busy Christmas season at the Silver Mart and my father had David and myself helping with the rush. I stayed in the back, wrapping packages and retrieving stock, while David was stationed in front of the store watching for shoplifters. This is astonishing, as David did not have what I would call an eagle eye; Helen Keller might have been a better lookout.

One afternoon, I was bringing some packages out to the front of the store when I heard my mother loudly question why there was an empty spot on one of the china shelves. This meant that a cup and saucer set that had been on display was missing. I knew the reason: David was on watch. It seems that moments earlier, a shabbily dressed young woman and her child were in the store, and my mother was sure she had taken it.

David and I ran from the store in search of the woman and the goods. We spotted her on the next block, scurrying away, with the child in tow. David ran up to her and stated that he knew she had stolen the teacup and to please give it back. He thoughtfully explained it was of no real use to her and that we needed it back because it was part of a full set of china. She denied having it and kept walking nervously away, at a quickened pace. I started to lose my patience with the situation as David walked beside her and continued to plead with her. The soft sell clearly wasn't working.

So finally, I stopped the woman and said to her, "I'll give you $20 for the cup and saucer."

She stopped dead in her tracks and quickly produced them from beneath her coat, then asked for her money. I snatched the items back and said, "Now get the hell out of here," clearly showing no intention to remunerate her for the theft. What was she going to do, call the police?

David felt badly for the woman and showed surprise that I had pulled a fast one on her, but I explained, as we walked back to the store, that paying her would only encourage more theft, which would be very problematic for my parents—especially if he continued to be the lookout.

ILISE

Ilise and I when we were dating

SHRIMP TEMPURA

Ilise and I were on our first official date. I met her in Manhattan with a plan to have dinner. We walked around for hours, checking the menus pasted in the windows of each restaurant. None of them suited her, so I assumed she was a picky eater. I started to question what I was getting myself into, as I was starving and Ilise did not seem any closer to making a decision. I finally had had enough and ushered her into a Mexican restaurant, not knowing or caring whether or not she liked Mexican food. As we were walking in, she questioned whether it was too expensive. It was at that moment I realized that she'd schlepped me to every restaurant in Manhattan not because of her appetite, but because of her concern over the cost and my ability to pay. As I write this twenty years later, I can safely say, that was the last time she ever checked a price.

On our second date, we decided to have Japanese food. We settled into our seats as the waiter handed us the menus. Ilise quickly decided on the shrimp tempura, but she had a request. "Is it possible to have the shrimp tempura, but without the breading?" She might as well have asked the dumbfounded waiter to split an atom. Giggling could be heard from the next table as I explained to Ilise that if they honored her request, a plate of plain, uncooked shrimp was all she could expect.

Ilise has never been shy about making her feelings known. If we were in Madison Square Garden and she was hot, Ilise would have no second thoughts about asking one of the attendants to turn up the air conditioning.

Also, how ironic it is that fourteen years after this memorable dinner in a Japanese restaurant, we would end up living in Tokyo for five wonderful years!

LARRY'S MUSTACHE

Larry was a close friend all through college, so Ilise and I would see him almost every day. One day towards the end of senior year, Larry showed up at my apartment, but he was missing something. His trademark moustache was gone! Larry without a mustache was like Jimmy Durante without a nose—it just wasn't right. He looked so different that I knew we could play a decent practical joke on Ilise.

A large group of friends were going to the movies that evening, so I explained to them that I planned to tell Ilise that Larry's brother Mark was visiting from the University of Pennsylvania for the weekend and would be joining us; Larry, unfortunately, couldn't make it as he had another engagement.

I saw Ilise later that day and mentioned that Larry's brother was in town and would be coming out with us that night. Ilise initially doubted the existence of Larry's brother, as she had never heard him mentioned before, but I persuaded her and she had no reason not to believe me. (In retrospect, maybe she had a very good reason.)

We showed up at the movies and the group was huddled around Larry, aka Mark. I went over and greeted him warmly, then turned and introduced him to Ilise. It was a joy to see the mixture of embarrassment and confusion on Ilise's face. She didn't want to say anything foolish, in case it really was Larry's brother, but she was befuddled. She turned to me for validation, but I just played along with Larry, who was able to keep a straight face the entire time. This convinced Ilise, who now started to pepper Mark with questions about his childhood with Larry, etc. This could have gone on forever, but we needed to disclose the joke in order to enjoy it. We all stepped away slowly as Larry, aka Mark, was prepped to make a romantic move on Ilise. But as he put his arm around her shoulder and professed his affection, he couldn't contain himself and burst out laughing. Needless to say, Ilise was not thrilled with me for making her the butt of a joke.

Tour d'Eiffel

Ilise at the Eiffel Tower

Ilise and I were newly married when we went on our first European vacation with our friends Jamie and Lee. Destination: Paris. One day we decided to check out the Eiffel Tower and see what all the fuss over the giant Erector Set was about. Since it is probably the most well-known landmark in all of France, it was only a trifle embarrassing when we exited the Metro and couldn't find it. We were a bunch of hapless tourists. That's when Ilise sprang to action and took the matter into her own hands. She brushed off her high school French and confidently strode up to a nearby couple.

"*Pardonnez moi, où est la Tour d'Eiffel, s'il vous plaît?*" Ilise inquired with conviction.

Much to her dismay, the gentleman responded in perfect English, "Sorry, we are from Trenton, New Jersey, and don't speak French, but if you are looking for the Eiffel Tower, it's right *there!*"

This was very embarrassing for Ilise and gave us a good laugh because we were no more than fifty yards from the landmark site, although we couldn't see it from where we stood.

FREDI

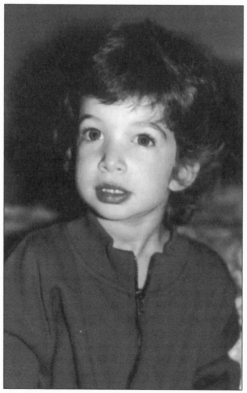

Fredi at three years old

A SPECIAL LADY

When my daughter Fredi was three years old, we took her to Stan Cohen's sixtieth birthday party. Stan has been my father's best friend for over forty years. It was a very nice afternoon affair, attended by family and friends. Stan's mother, a very fine woman, was there and we wanted to make sure Fredi knew that when we introduced her. So Ilise bent down to Fredi, and pointed over to Stan's mother, who was sitting across the room in an elegant red dress and was surrounded by a circle of fans. She said, "Fredi, do you see that woman over there, sitting down? She is a VERY special person. Do you know who she is?"

Fredi peered across the room and, with a look of excitement in her eyes, exclaimed, "Little Red Riding Hood?"

CAROLYN

Carolyn at seven years old

LOVE, CAROLYN

I must have committed a grave injustice to my daughter Carolyn one day because she was very upset with me. She was six years old, so it was probably something significant like allowing her only four chocolate candies for dessert. She stormed out of the kitchen and into her room. A few minutes later, as I was about to go look for her, Fredi came running into the kitchen, giggling, and told me to look on the message board to see what Carolyn had written. She had expressed her feelings quite honestly: "I Hate Daddy. Love Carolyn."

MY LITTLE EINSTEIN

I had the privilege of picking Fredi and Carolyn up at school one afternoon in Tokyo. I asked Fredi what she had learned in school that day and she gave me the standard answer— "Nothing." Carolyn was a little more animated and volunteered that she'd learned a lot. I said to Carolyn, "OK, if you learned so much today, then tell me, E equals mc...*what?*" hoping that the theory of relativity was part of her first-grade curriculum.

Seeing the quizzical look on her face, one of the mothers leaned over and in a heavy British accent whispered the answer in Carolyn's ear. Carolyn smiled confidently and proudly said, "SQUID!"

DALIAH

Fredi, Daliah, and Carolyn

Daliah Jill Bernstein was born in Tokyo on December 27th, 1998. She was born with a cataract in her right eye and received a lens transplant when she was only eight weeks old. To see my baby daughter have surgery so early in life is not something I would like to repeat. Since the operation, she has worn glasses to help correct her vision. She looks very cute in what might be the smallest pair of glasses in the world.

Many people are amazed to see an infant wearing spectacles and remark, "What does she need glasses for?"

Daliah's maternal grandmother has the best answer to this question: "For reading," she replies.

Some people actually accept this as a valid reason and nod their heads with understanding.

III
ME

THE STATUE OF LIBERTY

Of all the stories about my childhood, the visit to the Statue of Liberty when I was eight is the one most often repeated. My dad was only trying to do what fathers are supposed to do: Take the children out of the house to give Mom some peace and quiet. He planned on taking just David and myself to the Statue of Liberty.

Although it was probably less than five miles from our apartment in Brooklyn, it was a major undertaking. The day started off on the wrong foot. Actually, feet. My parents insisted we dress nicely since it was a Jewish holiday. I wanted to wear sneakers, but they forced me to wear black leather dress shoes; I lost that battle. I was in a bad mood and wanted to make my displeasure known.

As we approached the ferry, I told my father I was not going on it. He tried the old scare tactic and said, "Fine. Stay here by yourself," and boarded the ferry with David in tow.

I stood on the dock, with no real plan of action, and saw that my father and brother had reached the top deck. My father leaned over and yelled to me, "Steven, get up here already!" and threw a balled-up ticket onto the dock for me.

I didn't budge. A few seconds later, the warning whistle blew, which meant the ferry was about to depart. My father looked panicked as he tried all his best methods of persuasion to get me on the boat. First came the pleasant cajoling with promises of toys. No luck. Then came the reality threat— "If you don't get on now, you will be left there all by yourself and you'll get lost!"

For some reason, this failed to scare me. I must have really hated those shoes. Then, as the last whistle blew, out came the final and furious, maniacal screaming of a desperate man. I could literally see the veins popping out of his neck as his crimson face glared down at me. "STEVEN, I'M TELLING YOU NOW, YOU GET ON THIS GODDAMN BOAT OR I'M GONNA KILL YOU!"

This swayed me. I reluctantly got on the boat and went up to the top deck. To my father's credit, he kept his distance from me. If the situation were reversed, I might have thrown a child overboard. Every time I moved closer to my father, he moved away. He was determined to teach me a lesson. As the ferry docked on Liberty Island, David got off the boat with an armful of candy, toys, and soda. I got nothing. As we walked to Miss Liberty, I was about twenty steps behind them. I was afraid to go inside, as I didn't think my father would pay for me, so I sat on a park bench the whole time, playing with a puzzle that I'd fortunately brought along. I finally saw them leave the monument. David was holding a statuette, postcards, and anything else my father could purchase along the way. The only new things I possessed were my dress shoes. We walked back to the ferry and finally got across to the other side.

My father had not said one word to me since he'd screamed at me from the top deck. We got into the car. Just before my father pulled out, he turned to me in the backseat and finally spoke, slowly and threateningly, as he was clearly in control now. "When we get home...you're dead!"

I don't recall any particularly brutal punishment that evening. Luckily for me, even my father laughs about it now. To this day, I have never been inside the Statue of Liberty.

A DEFINING MOMENT

A defining moment in my life occurred when I was about ten years old. I was fooling around outside when I picked up a very large rock and decided to see how high I could throw it. I crouched down, holding the boulder in front of me, and sprang up, heaving it high into the air. I remember, vividly, looking straight up to see the rock suspended in the air above my head, ready to submit to gravitational forces. This would not be pleasant. In a panic, I lunged forward. I felt it skim past my back and hit the ground with a thud. It was at that moment that I understood I was responsible for my own actions and that the consequences of these actions would determine my future health, success, and happiness.

I LOVE TO WIN

Another watershed experience took place when I was twelve years old. We were in summer camp and our group was scattered along a stream hunting for crayfish. There was always a big competition to see who could catch the biggest crayfish.

I sat crouched on my favorite rock, peering into the clear water. It seemed that I was not destined to win that day, for there was nothing in the water, except what appeared to be a small black stone. Our counselor gave us the ten-minute warning to finish up and I was getting anxious, as my friends had already caught some crayfish. I hated to lose, but I certainly did not want to be shut out! With nothing happening in the water, I unconsciously decided to poke the small black stone.

As I touched it, the stone sprang out of the mud. It was actually the back of a very large crayfish, right under my nose the whole time! It scurried under a rock. I was mad at myself for having watched it for so long without trying to see what it was. The counselor announced it was time to leave. I was in a panic. If I could find this crayfish, I would certainly be the winner that day and maybe for the whole summer, as it was rather large.

Just as my counselor prodded me to get going, I saw it emerge from under the rock I was sitting on. With two fingers, I picked him up and put him in the paper cup I carried with me. I was the clear winner and the envy of my friends that day.

I cannot even imagine picking up a crayfish today. It's interesting that things like bugs, crayfish, snakes, and spiders held no fear for me as a child, but today I would be standing on a chair in fright. That day, I learned not to let opportunities slip by without at least trying—and sometimes those opportunities are right in front of your nose the whole time.

KNOWING WHEN TO GIVE IN

Me at sixteen

When I felt too old to work at summer camp but too young for a real job, I decided to go down to Wildwood, New Jersey, with my friend Daniel to seek employment. We looked around the boardwalk and finally found jobs at a large variety store selling T-shirts, hats, sandals, etc. I was responsible for the hat section, which was in the front of the store. This was ideal; the front was open and right on the boardwalk, so I could check out the sights when I wasn't busy. Daniel got stuck at the back of the store in the highly lucrative T-shirt section and wasn't happy about it. I explained to him that girls bought more T-shirts than hats. That seemed to brighten his spirits a bit.

We worked there a total of four days and it rained for every one of them. When it rains on the boardwalk, there isn't much traffic. I would have renamed it bored-walk. On what turned out to be my final day of a less-than-stellar retailing career, an extremely large black man came in and started trying on hats. I was watching him out of the corner of my eye as he selected a hat and started to walk around the store with it perched on his head. I had my eye on him. Nobody steals from the hat section under my watch! Sure enough, after a few minutes I spotted him making his exit from the store.

I walked up to him and said, "Excuse me sir, aren't you going to pay for that hat?"

He took a step closer to me. I looked straight up at him as he hovered over me like an umbrella. He put his large hands on my shoulders and said confidently, "I walked in with it, right?"

Who was I to argue? "Yes, and it looks very good on you," I squeaked, as he turned and left the store.

RESERVATIONS

I was a sophomore at Boston University and it was close to semester break. Since I didn't possess a car, I would often fly back to New York to see my family. So I called the airline and when a woman answered, I simply explained that I wanted to make a reservation. She responded with surprise, "YOU WHAT?"

I repeated a little more forcefully that I wanted to make a reservation and could she please help me. She started to laugh uncontrollably and said, "Honey, we don't take reservations!"

I had never heard of an airline refusing to take reservations. Something didn't make sense so I checked the number with her. I had inadvertently dialed the Boston City Morgue.

IT'S A BOY!

My oldest daughter, Fredi, was born on November 11, 1988. We had spent the whole day at the hospital and she finally arrived at 10:21 at night. Our friends Ward and Tara were having a baby and their due date was around the same time. When I called to tell them about Fredi, Ward said that Tara's water had broken and they were on their way to the hospital.

I remember driving home alone that night along streets that were deserted. I turned on the radio and the song "Suite Judy Blue Eyes" by CSNY came on. It was one of the happiest moments of my life. By the time I got home it was about 2 a.m. and I was exhausted. The ring of the phone awakened me at 6 a.m. Groggily, I answered it, trying to sound awake but with little success. Ward yelled excitedly, "It's a boy!"

I responded in the caustic way we usually spoke to each other, "No, it was a girl, you idiot!"

He hesitated for a second and then snapped, "Not you, me, you moron!"

It finally sank in. Just six hours after Ilise delivered our daughter, Tara delivered a boy at the same hospital with the same doctor.

FORE!

It was the summer of 1993 and I had been fortunate enough to be invited to watch a practice round of the U.S. Open Golf Tournament, being held at Baltusrol Country Club. All of golf's major names were there, including Jack Nicklaus, Greg Norman, and Fred Couples. The pro from my golf club also qualified for the tournament and I thought it would be fun to watch him play the round.

When I entered the course, I was handed a sheet of paper which listed the tee times for the day's practice round and a map of the holes. I scanned it and soon found out that the foursome I wanted to watch had started about one hour earlier. As I studied the map, trying to calculate which hole they would currently be playing, and where it was located, I walked quickly through the rough.

All of a sudden, I heard the crowd gasp. I stopped dead in my tracks as my foot came to rest on something hard and round. I was standing directly on a golf ball that had been hit from the tee and trickled into the rough. There was a circle of people around me, with looks of shock and disgust on their faces.

I didn't stay around long enough to see who had hit the ball, as I was extremely embarrassed. Thank heavens, it was only a practice round or else the media coverage would have been brutal. My only thought was, Don't these kinds of things usually happen to other people?

IV

WORK

THE MEETING FROM HELL

Salomon Brothers

Here was the big chance. My boss asked me to attend a meeting with the president of a major Japanese insurance company and his key executives. They were coming to Salomon Brothers to see John Gutfreund, our chairman and CEO, and Tom Strauss, our president. Being a very junior salesperson, this was my first experience participating in such a high-profile meeting. I prepared for it as a climber would for Mt. Everest. I studied every market, knew the yields of every government bond in the world, tracked all the major currencies, brushed up on global events, and was able to recite the financial statement of this client verbatim.

All for naught. I sat through the meeting shaking with fear, but not a single question was posed to me. It occurred to me, later on, that this meeting had had nothing to do with me and maybe I am not necessarily the center of the universe all the time.

As the conversation progressed, it became obvious that I was as important to this gathering as the coffee table in front of us, maybe less so. This calmed me. At the conclusion of the meeting, I felt the need to provide some meaningful role, albeit a small one. I decided to open the office door for their departure. Rising from my chair, I made a quick, hard turn around my armchair and reached for the door.

MISTAKE!

The elegant antique end table, which was situated right next to my chair and had existed quite nicely for over 150 years, was soon lying defenseless on the carpet, nursing its injured leg like a Thoroughbred waiting for the fatal bullet, its contents strewn all over my CEO's brilliant white carpet.

Let me describe the scene a little more precisely: Before my mad rush to the door, Gutfreund's freshly lit cigar had been resting in a marble ashtray next to me. As the table fell, the cigar decided to tattoo the alabaster carpet with its ash and the ashtray, which was round, felt the need to circle the room. My thoughts about how to redeem the situation were clouded with indecision about which item to salvage first. The table was the most expensive, but the cigar was doing the most damage, yet the ashtray was definitely the most mobile. Unfortunately, I chose the fourth option, which was to stand motionless, mouth agape. Strauss dove for the ashtray; Gutfreund, in his inimitable style, crushed the cigar beneath his loafer; the president of Daiichi Life delicately lifted the broken table to an upright state that was now far from level.

How do you placate your parents, who funded your education for over twenty years, when you are trying to explain that you were fired from a plum Wall Street job because of a lapse in spatial judgment? "But Dad, I knew the dollar exchange rate of every currency in the world— go ahead, ask me!"

Never before had I received (or worn) a pink slip, but I expected it to arrive as soon as I returned to my desk. My boss, to his credit, enjoyed my misery and must have known that nothing would come of the extremely embarrassing situation. As I write this, my career at Salomon has surpassed sixteen years and has thus far been free of pink slips, which was not the case for Mr. Gutfreund and Mr. Strauss.

THE INCIDENT

Of all the funny stories, books, and articles that have been written about Salomon Brothers, nothing compares with this as-yet-unpublished episode from the old Salomon Brothers. Some names have been changed to protect the not-so-innocent.

First, the background: Alan was the clerk on the commercial paper desk for Salomon Brothers in the mid-1980s. This meant he was the lowest of the low. Alan was very good at his job and was liked by all traders and salespeople, but he was also very easy to poke fun at. Alan was short, plump, and had a high-pitched, nasal voice, not unlike that of a cartoon character. He always wore a pair of ugly brown shoes to work, no matter what color suit he had on. Johnny was one of the senior commercial paper traders and a practical joker. If he wasn't poking fun at Alan, then he was probably sleeping.

One afternoon, Johnny got a call from nature. He headed to the bathroom, newspaper in hand, for a stint that was destined to be on the long side. As Johnny was finishing up his business, he glanced over to the floor of the adjoining stall and noticed Alan's ugly brown shoes, hiding under a bunched-up pair of pants. Not one to pass up an opportunity, Johnny readied himself for a quick exit and went into action.

He reached under the wall, grabbed Alan's shoe, and tried to wrestle it from his foot, to take back to the desk as his trophy. Alan would not give up his sole so easily. He writhed in a fit of frenzy as Johnny pulled and twisted his shoe, to no avail. Johnny finally gave up and cackled uncontrollably as he ran from the stall, leaving Alan to contemplate why his few minutes of peace had been seriously invaded.

Johnny hustled back to the desk with a smirk on his face, ready to share a laugh with the other traders, at Alan's expense. There was only one problem—and it was a big one: When Johnny returned to the desk, Alan was sitting in his seat. A chill ran up Johnny's spine as he asked Alan one question, to which he already knew the answer: "Tell me you were in the bathroom just now," he pleaded. No such luck.

Johnny sat down in his seat and slumped as far down as possible, keeping an eye on the bathroom door. Who could it have been? His only hope was that it was someone with less stature in the firm than Alan, which was nearly impossible. Moments later, the bathroom door was flung open with fury as our illustrious chief economist and vice chairman, Henry Kaufman, bolted onto the trading floor in a rage, wearing his own pair of ugly brown shoes. He glared piercingly at every person with hatred, ready to change the course of someone's life. Johnny stayed trapped in his bunker, shaking like a leaf, as he waited for his pursuer to retreat.

To my knowledge, Dr. Henry Kaufman, possibly the most famous economist in the history of Wall Street, never found out who the culprit was, and unless he reads this book, probably never will.

HENRY, TOO

I also had what I like to call an "HK" experience, although it was much less confrontational. I was a freshly minted salesperson straight out of the training program. My boss asked me to call Henry's office to get our estimate of the unemployment number. This monthly piece of economic data is crucial for the markets. Fortunes are normally gained or lost on its release.

I was well aware of the importance of this number. I also knew that our estimate of this number was something every salesperson should always have ingrained in their head. As a novice salesman, there was no choice but to follow my boss's instructions. I called Henry Kaufman's office, certain that his secretary would answer and easily provide me with the information.

I didn't know, at that time, that secretaries rarely show up to work before nine a.m. At seven a.m., which is when I needed the answer, they're still teasing their hair, which left Henry Kaufman in the awkward position of answering his own phone.

Hearing his familiar voice on the other end of the line snap at me "HENRY!" sent a wave of panic through my bones.

I decided the best thing to do was act like a senior salesperson even though at that moment sucking on a pacifier and crying for mommy seemed preferable. I cleared my throat and said confidently to Dr. Doom, "Henry, can you tell me what our estimate for unemployment is today?"

Maybe he thought I was testing him. Maybe he couldn't believe that there was someone in the world who didn't know his forecast. Whatever the reason, I could sense the indignation on the other end of the phone. Henry growled and then angrily bellowed the words, "WHO IS THIS?" so loudly that I was instantly reminded of the Wizard of Oz, at the sound of whose voice the cowardly lion panicked and jumped out of the window. Since I was sitting in the middle of the trading floor, the window exit would have been a difficult choice but not entirely out of the question. Once again, I was faced with a career-impacting decision. I could identify myself and hope for the best or I could give him a false name and hope he never checked. I thought for a second about his question and realized immediately what course of action I should take.

I hung up.

If I'd had more nerve, I would have calmly said, "I'm the guy who tried to rip your shoe off in the bathroom."

THE PIG NEXT TO YOU...

My friend Andrew completed Salomon's training program and was assigned to the mortgage trading desk. In case you never read the book *Liar's Poker*, this was a wild bunch of guys. They were infamous for being a brash group of traders who would gorge themselves with junk food on a daily basis. The combined weight of the mortgage traders was always a hotly debated topic. The co-heads of the desk, Mike and Mason, led by example, as they could easily be described as full-figured men. Andrew reported to the desk and was ordered to sit in the only open seat, which happened to be right between the two co-heads. His job: answering the phones. Any time the phone lit up, Andrew was to forward the call to a more important person on the desk. He spent all day fielding calls, with his bosses berating him left and right.

Later that day, Andrew was sitting between the two men who would decide the path of his future career on Wall Street. He picked up the phone and a caller demanded, "Let me speak to the pig next to you."

Andrew responded thoughtfully and quickly answered, "Which one?"

Although it was a good question, there were some serious complications. The caller was Mason, two seats away, using a private line to reach Mike. Andrew quickly realized his mistake and glanced nervously to his right, as Mason growled, "You're dead!"

Suspenders

Another funny situation on the mortgage trading desk occurred when an investment banker from the corporate finance department made the unfortunate error of walking by the traders on a not-so-busy afternoon. Since he was wearing the standard-issue suspenders that investment bankers seem to think make them look professional, the mortgage traders took offense immediately. Their unwritten rule was that anyone who came within the vicinity of the mortgage trading desk would have their suspenders cut. Most salespeople and traders at the firm were aware of this and preferred the more casual "belt" look anyway.

The banker walked right into the lair, unaware of the discontent he was causing. One of the traders immediately got up from his chair, grabbed the back of the banker's suspenders, and cut them in half. Needless to say, the banker was furious. He protested vehemently while everyone hooted around him. He retaliated by grabbing the suit jacket off the attacker's chair and ripping it violently into pieces.

The whole desk howled with laughter, yet the trader was unfazed. It seems that he had been sitting at the desk of a colleague who was out to lunch at the time. His own suit jacket was safely hanging in the closet.

V
EPILOGUE

Morty

I thought it would be a good idea to send my father a draft copy of this book, to get his reaction. Sometimes my ideas are better if they're left just as ideas.

I sent him the book when he was visiting my brother David in Hawaii. David described the scene to me with relish: My father sat stone-faced in the chair and read the book from cover to cover. He showed no reaction to any of the stories, even the ones about him. He finished the book, closed it, and placed it on the table with no comment at all.

David finally broke down and asked him, "So, did you like the book?"

My father peered up at him and gave his standard repetitive response, "Did I like the book? Did I like the book." He sighed and then remarked, with an air of certainty, "I would have picked different stories."

When David pointed out that it is not a biography of Morty Bernstein but, in fact, a book written about events in the life of his son Steven, he interrupted and qualified his comment—"I'm just sayin', I would have picked different stories."